Music Superstars

RIHANNA

ARIEL FACTOR BIRDOFF

TORQUE

TORQUE, AN IMPRINT OF BELLWETHER MEDIA BY FLUTTERBEE

Torque brims with excitement perfect for thrill-seekers of all kinds. Discover daring survival skills, explore uncharted worlds, and marvel at mighty engines and extreme sports. In *Torque* books, anything can happen. Are you ready?

This edition first published in 2026 by Bellwether Media, Inc.

For information regarding permission, write to Bellwether Media, Inc., Attention: Permissions Department, 3500 American Blvd W, Suite 150, Bloomington, MN 55431.
Library of Congress Cataloging-in-Publication Data is available at www.loc.gov or upon request from the publisher.

ISBN: 9798893048308 (hardcover)
ISBN: 9798893049305 (ebook)

Editor: Rachael Barnes Designer: Josh Brink

Printed in the United States of America, North Mankato, MN.

TABLE OF CONTENTS

SUPER BOWL SUPERSTAR

All eyes are on Rihanna at the 2023 Super Bowl Halftime Show. It is Rihanna's first live performance in five years!

Rihanna wears an **iconic** red jumpsuit. She stands out surrounded by dancers in white suits. She sings many of her hit songs, including "Only Girl in the World" and "Umbrella." The show ends with fireworks!

WHO IS RIHANNA?

Rihanna is a world-famous pop and R&B singer. She has won many awards and set world records! Her hit songs and powerful voice are famous around the world.

RIHANNA

Birthday	Hometown	Types of Music	First Hit
February 20, 1988	St. Michael parish, Barbados	pop, R&B	"Pon de Replay"

Rihanna is also an actor and successful businesswoman. She has her own fashion and beauty lines.

ISLAND GIRL

Robyn Rihanna Fenty is from a small island in the Caribbean called Barbados. She grew up in a small village. She listened to a lot of music. Her favorite **genres** were reggae, hip-hop, and R&B.

RIHANNA AT AGE 11

RIHANNA'S CHILDHOOD HOME

A STREET NAMED RIHANNA

The street that Rihanna grew up on is now named Rihanna Drive!

She loved playing at the beach with her two younger brothers. She often pretended to be a famous singer. She even used her hairbrush as a microphone.

Rihanna loved singing. She performed in and won her high school talent show. Afterwards, she started a band with two of her friends.

RIHANNA PERFORMING IN 2005

FAVORITES

Accessories
diamond jewelry

Dessert
chocolate ice cream

Sport
basketball

Colors
brown and green

In 2004, the band performed for an American producer. He saw Rihanna's talent. Soon Rihanna left Barbados and moved to the United States. In 2005, she signed with the **record label** Def Jam.

"PON DE REPLAY"

Rihanna had huge success with her 2005 **debut**. She **released** her first single! "Pon de Replay" reached number two on the ***Billboard*** Hot 100 chart. Her first album, *Music of the Sun*, came out soon after.

Her second album, *A Girl Like Me*, came out the next year. The song "SOS" was Rihanna's first number one hit!

For her third album, *Good Girl Gone Bad*, Rihanna **collaborated** with Timbaland and Justin Timberlake. Her song "Umbrella" won a **Grammy Award**! She is the first person from Barbados to win a Grammy.

2008 GRAMMY AWARDS PERFORMANCE

AWARDS

as of November 2025

4 MTV Video Music Awards

3 NAACP Image Awards

12 *Billboard* Music Awards

9 Grammy Awards

13 American Music Awards

Rihanna then re-released the album in 2008 with three new songs. The original album and *Good Girl Gone Bad: Reloaded* are still some of her most popular music.

Rihanna started working with other artists on their songs! She is featured in Maroon 5's "If I Never See Your Face Again." She recorded and released more albums, including *Rated R* in 2009 and *Loud* in 2010.

RIHANNA AND MAROON 5

RECORD BREAKER

At 23 years old, Rihanna was the youngest artist to reach 10 number one *Billboard* hits!

Her sixth album, *Talk That Talk*, featured the hit song "We Found Love." The music video for the song won Rihanna another Grammy!

Unapologetic came out in 2012. *ANTI* came out in 2016. Rihanna then decided to take a break from releasing her own music.

Rihanna worked on one song in 2022. "Lift Me Up" was created for the movie *Black Panther: Wakanda Forever*. It won an NAACP Image Award for Outstanding Music Video. In 2023, Rihanna performed at the Super Bowl Halftime Show.

TIMELINE

– 2005 –

Rihanna releases her first single, "Pon de Replay"

– 2008 –

Rihanna wins her first Grammy Award for "Umbrella"

RIHANNA PERFORMING IN 2016

TRIPLE THREAT

Rihanna sings and dances! She has also acted in movies such as *Battleship* and *Ocean's 8*.

– 2013 –

Rihanna wins a Grammy Award for the "We Found Love" music video

– 2017 –

Rihanna starts her makeup company, Fenty Beauty

– 2023 –

"Lift Me Up" wins an NAACP Image Award for Outstanding Music Video

THE RIHANNA NAVY

Rihanna fans get their name from her "G4L" **lyrics**. They are "an army, better yet a navy." The Navy loves Rihanna, and she loves them back. They share inside jokes, birthday wishes, and milestones.

PLAYLIST

"Pon de Replay"
(2005)

"SOS"
(2006)

"Don't Stop the Music"
(2007)

"We Found Love"
(2011)

"Diamonds"
(2012)

"Lift Me Up"
(2022)

Rihanna is an incredible musical artist. Her fans cannot wait to see what she does next!

GLOSSARY

Billboard—related to a well-known music news magazine and website that ranks songs and albums

collaborated—worked with others to create something

debut—a first appearance or release

genres—categories for types of music

Grammy Award—an award given by the Recording Academy of the United States for an achievement in music; Grammy Awards are also called Grammys.

iconic—widely recognized and admired

lyrics—the words of a song

record label—a company that sells music

released—made music available for listening

TO LEARN MORE

AT THE LIBRARY

Andreoni, Regina. *Rihanna: A Little Golden Book Biography.* New York, N.Y.: Penguin Random House, 2025.

Birdoff, Ariel Factor. *Bad Bunny*. Minneapolis, Minn.: Bellwether Media, 2025.

Birdoff, Ariel Factor. *Beyoncé*. Minneapolis, Minn.: Bellwether Media, 2025.

ON THE WEB

FACTSURFER

Factsurfer.com gives you a safe, fun way to find more information.

1. Go to www.factsurfer.com.
2. Enter "Rihanna" into the search box and click 🔍.
3. Select your book cover to see a list of related content.

INDEX

The images in this book are reproduced through the courtesy of: Kansas City Chiefs/ AP Images, front cover; Joe Seer, p. 3; PA Images/ Alamy Stock Photo, pp. 4-5, 5; A.RICARDO, p. 6; Dimitrios Kambouris/ Staff/ Getty Images, p. 7 (top); Monica Schipper/ Staff/ Getty Images, p. 7 (bottom); ARCHIVIO GBB/ Alamy Stock Photo, p. 8; Imago/ Alamy Stock Photo, pp. 8-9; ZUMA Press, Inc./ Alamy Stock Photo, p. 10; Abaca Press/ Alamy Stock Photo, p. 11; NPDESIGNTOP, p. 11 (accessories); Moni 8004, p. 11 (dessert); grey_and, p. 11 (sport); Elena11, p. 11 (colors); Theo Wargo/ Staff/ Getty Images, pp. 12-13; John Ricard/ Contributor/ Getty Images, p. 13; ROBYN BECK/ Staff/ Getty Images, pp. 14-15; Christopher Polk/ Contributor/ Getty Images, pp. 16-17; John Shearer/ Staff/ Getty Images, p. 17; Doug Peters/ Alamy Stock Photo, pp. 18-19; Def Jam/ Wikipedia, pp. 19 (2005, 2008), 21 (Pon de Replay, SOS, Don't Stop the Music, We Found Love, Diamonds); Gerald Zaffuts, p. 19 (2013); Westbury Road/ Wikipedia, pp. 19 (2023), 21 (Lift Me Up); Jason Kempin/ Staff/ Getty Images, p. 20; Icon Sportswire/ Contributor/ Getty Images, pp. 20-21; Fred Duval, p. 23.